5 Saxes + Rhythm Section

Thaddeus

JERRY DODGION

Recorded by JERRY DODGION
on *THE JOY OF SAX*

Love And Smiles Music (LSM 101)

JERRY DODGION, alto sax
BRAD LEALI, alto sax
FRANK WESS, tenor sax
DAN BLOCK, tenor sax
JAY BRANDFORD, baritone sax
MIKE LeDONNE, piano
DENNIS IRWIN, bass
JOE FARNSWORTH, drums

Recorded October 2, 2003

CD available at www.JerryDodgion.com

INSTRUMENTATION
1st part: **Alto Sax 1**
2nd part: **Alto Sax 2**
3rd part: **Tenor Sax 1**
4th part: **Tenor Sax 2**
5th part: **Baritone Sax**
Rhythm Section: **Piano, Bass, Drums**
FULL SCORE

A DON SICKLER PRODUCTION

Second Floor Music

Exclusively Distributed By
HAL•LEONARD® CORPORATION
7777 W. BLUEMOUND RD. P.O. BOX 13819 MILWAUKEE, WI 53213

Thaddeus

JERRY DODGION

* suggested rhythmic approach to accompany soloist

engraved by Osho Endo

Alt 1
Alt 2
Ten 1
Ten 2
Bari
Bass
Dr
mf
mf
mf
mf
mf
mp
13
C
mp
mp
mp
mp
mp
C
17
Thaddeus

Alt 1
Alt 2
Ten 1
Ten 2
Bari
Bass
Dr
mf
21
8va
loco
D
Alt 1
Alt 2
Ten 1
Ten 2
Bari
Bass
Dr
mf
pp
p gradual cresc.
25

double time feel
double time feel
double time feel
double time feel
double time feel
with saxes
double time feel
double time feel
Alt 1
Alt 2
Ten 1
Ten 2
Bari
Bass
Dr
29
full
full
full
full
full
mf
mf
mf
mf
mf
sub. p
sub. p
sub. p
sub. p
sub. p
sfz
sfz
sfz
sfz
sub. p
sub. p
sub. p
sub. p
sub. p
solo freely
mp melody cue
Alt 1
Alt 2
Ten 1
Ten 2
Bari
Pno
Bass
Dr
mp
pp
sfz
p
32
Thaddeus

E
Bm7b5 Bbmaj7 Bb7#5 (b9)   A7#5(b9) Abm7b5   Gmaj7 Gbmaj7 Fmaj7 Emaj7 Ebmaj7   A7#5(b9)
Pno
Bass
Bm7b5 Bbmaj7 Bb7#5 (b9)   A7#5(b9) Abm7b5   Gmaj7 Gbmaj7 Fmaj7 Emaj7 Ebmaj7   A7#5(b9)
mf
Dr
38
p
Fmaj7/G Emaj7/F#   Ebmaj7/F F7(b9)   Ebmaj7 Dm7 Cm7 Bbmaj7 A7
Pno
Fmaj7/G Emaj7/F#   Ebmaj7/F F7(b9)   Ebmaj7 Dm7 Cm7 Bbmaj7 A7
Bass
Dr
42
F
Dm7b5 Dbmaj7 Db7#5 (b9)   C7#5(b9) Bm7b5   Bbmaj7   Abmaj7 Dbmaj7 C7#5(b9)
Pno
Dm7b5 Dbmaj7 Db7#5 (b9)   C7#5(b9) Bm7b5   Bbmaj7   Abmaj7 Dbmaj7 C7#5(b9)
Bass
Dr
46
* suggested rhythmic approach to accompany soloist

Thaddeus

Pno
Bass
Dr
Fm9/Bb Em9/A Ebm9/Ab Ab7(b9) Gbmaj7 Fm7 Ebm7 Db
Bass solo
solo (melody)
50
G
Bbdim(maj7) Bdim(maj7) Cdim(maj7) C#dim(maj7)
54
B7 Bb7 A7 Ab7 Gm F#9(13)
Bbm7b5
58
Thaddeus

H
Alt 1
Alt 2
Ten 1
Ten 2
Bari
Pno
Bass
Dr
play
8vb
p
mp
mf
pp
61
Alt 1
Alt 2
Ten 1
Ten 2
Bari
Pno
Bass
Dr
p gradual cresc.
p gradual cresc.
p gradual cresc.
p gradual cresc.
p gradual cresc.
mf
mf
mf
65
Thaddeus

double time feel
Alt 1
Alt 2
Ten 1
Ten 2
Bari
Piano
with saxes
Bass
mf
Dr
67
proudly
mp
mf
sub.p
sfp
6
Pno
Bass
mp
pp
to sticks
p
69

Thaddeus

Alt 1
Alt 2
Ten 1
Ten 2
Bari
Pno
Bass
Dr
"time" on hi-hat
75
Alt 1
Alt 2
Ten 1
Ten 2
Bari
Pno
Bass
Dr
81
gradual cresc.
(8vb)
8vb
Thaddeus

Alt 1
Alt 2
Ten 1
Ten 2
Bari
Pno
Bass
Dr
mp
mp
mp
mp
mp
(8vb)
85
mf
mf
mf
mf
mf
Alt 1
Alt 2
Ten 1
Ten 2
Bari
Pno
Bass
Dr
mf
mf
mf
mf
mf
mf
mf
mf
mf
(8vb)
89

Thaddeus

Alt 1
Alt 2
Ten 1
Ten 2
Bari
Pno
Bass
Dr
(8vb)
mp
mp
mp
mp
f
f
f
f
f
92
vamp until cue
vamp until cue
mf
mf
(mf)
mf
95
Thaddeus

on cue
tr
mf
Alt 1
Alt 2
Ten 1
Ten 2
Bari
on cue
Pno
Bass
Dr
101
105
Thaddeus

14

Alt 1
Alt 2
Ten 1
Ten 2
Bari
Pno
Bass
Dr
109
Alt 1
Alt 2
Ten 1
Ten 2
Bari
Pno
Bass
Dr
"time" on hi-hat
113
Thaddeus

Alt 1
Alt 2
Ten 1
Ten 2
Bari
Pno
Bass
Dr
117
"time" continues on hi-hat
124
Thaddeus

Alt 1
Alt 2
Ten 1
Ten 2
Bari
Pno
Bass
Dr
ff
pedal
130
Alt 1
Alt 2
Ten 1
Ten 2
Bari
Pno
Bass
Dr
8va
mf
mf
mf
let ring
no cut off
let ring
no cut off
134
Thaddeus

ALTO SAX 1
Recorded on THE JOY OF SAX / Jerry Dodgion (Love and Smiles Music LSM 101)
Thaddeus
JERRY DODGION 
Rubato
Solo (with Piano)
A
mf
set tempo (♩ = ca. 62)
B lead
pp
mp
C
mp
mf
D
mf
pp
p gradual cresc.
double time feel
full
mf
sub. p
sfz
sub. p
Copyright © 1988, 2003 SECOND FLOOR MUSIC
International Copyright Secured   All Rights Reserved   Made in U.S.A.
engraved by Osho Endo

E Piano solo
F
G Bass solo
H
double time feel
proudly
p
mf
pp
p gradual cresc.
mf
mp
mf
sub. p
sf p
mf
mf
p
mp
mf
mf
f

ALTO SAX 1 page 3 - Thaddeus
vamp until cue
on cue
mf
tr
tr
tr

Recorded on THE JOY OF SAX / Jerry Dodgion (Love and Smiles Music LSM 101)

ALTO SAX 2

Thaddeus

JERRY DODGION

engraved by Osho Endo

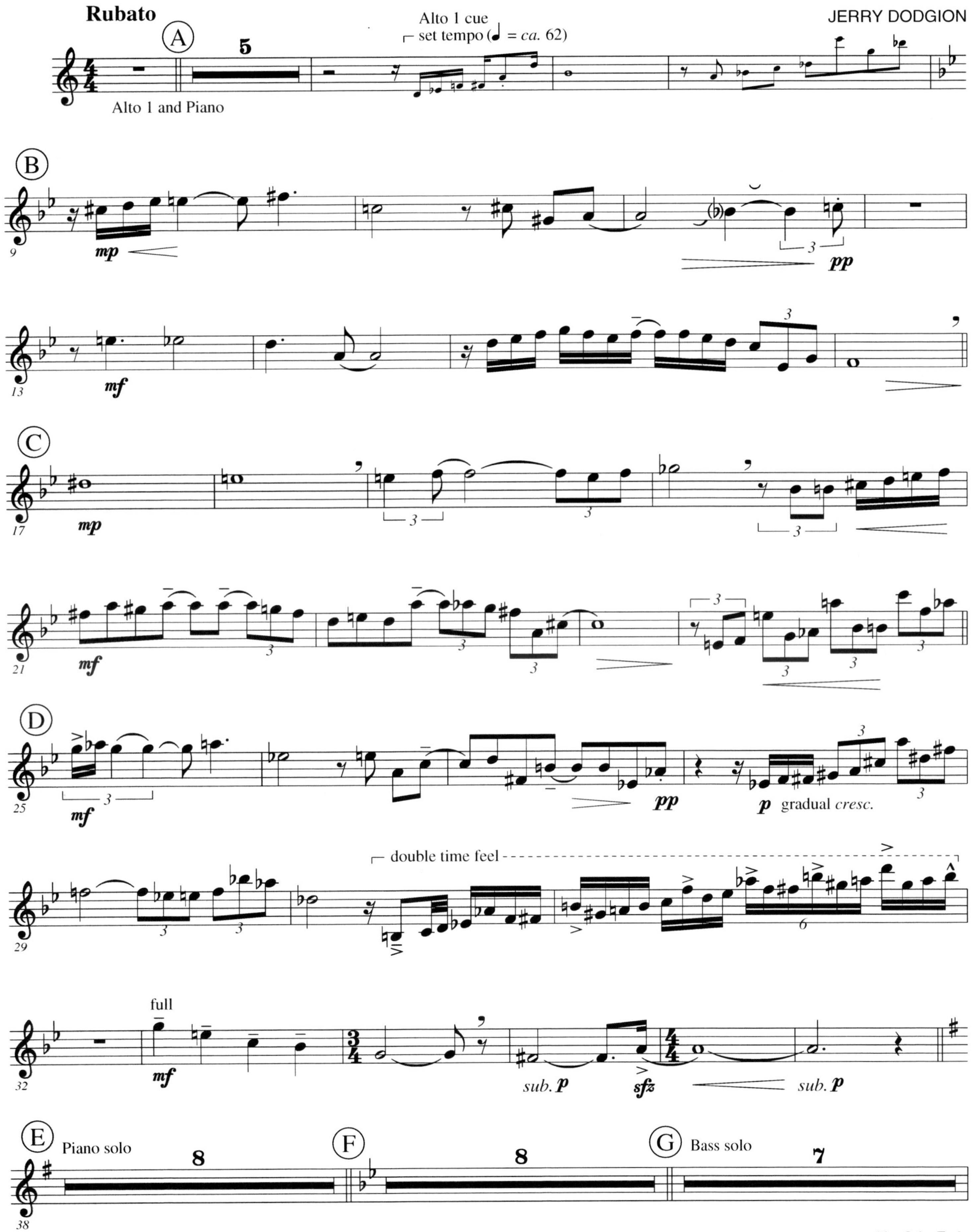

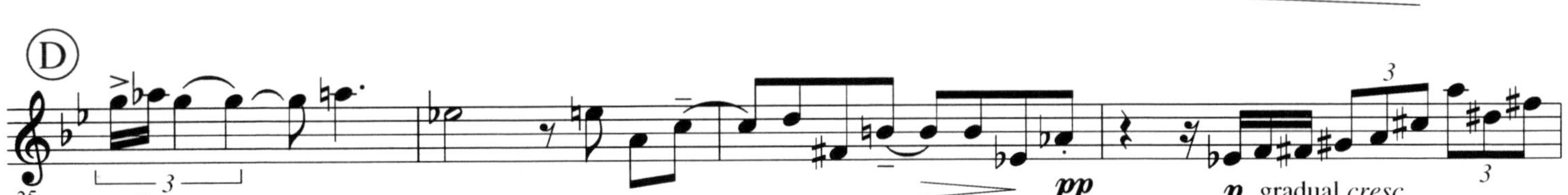

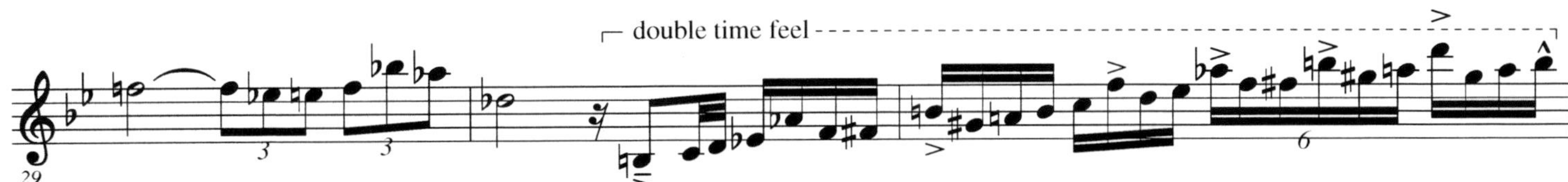

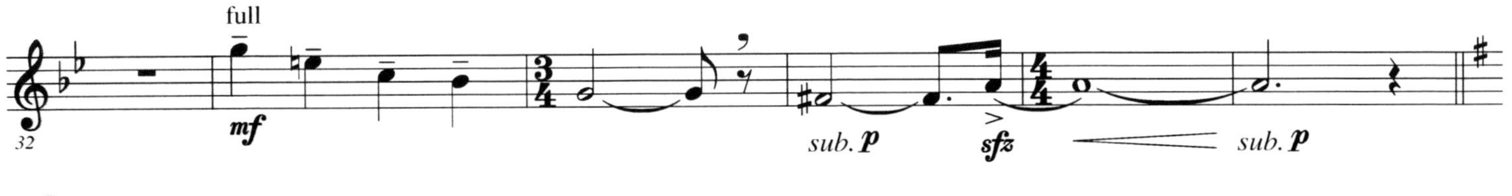

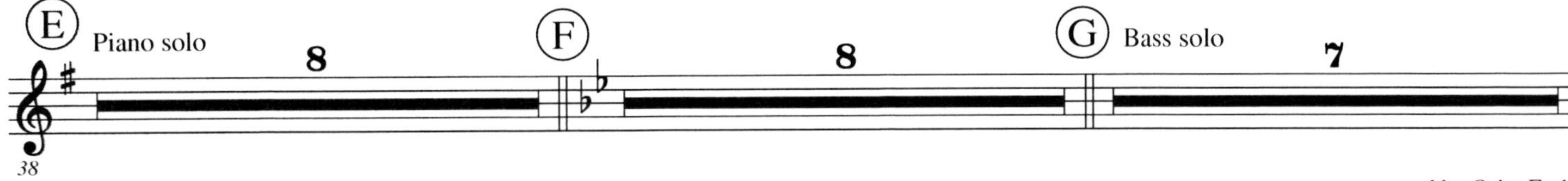

H
double time feel
proudly
p gradual cresc.
mf
mp
mf
sub. p
sf p
p
mp
mf
mp
mf
mf
p
pp
f

ALTO SAX 2 page 3 - Thaddeus
vamp until cue
on cue
tr
mf
95
101
105
3
tr
tr
109
113
117
122
127
2
132

Thaddeus

JERRY DODGION

engraved by Osho Endo

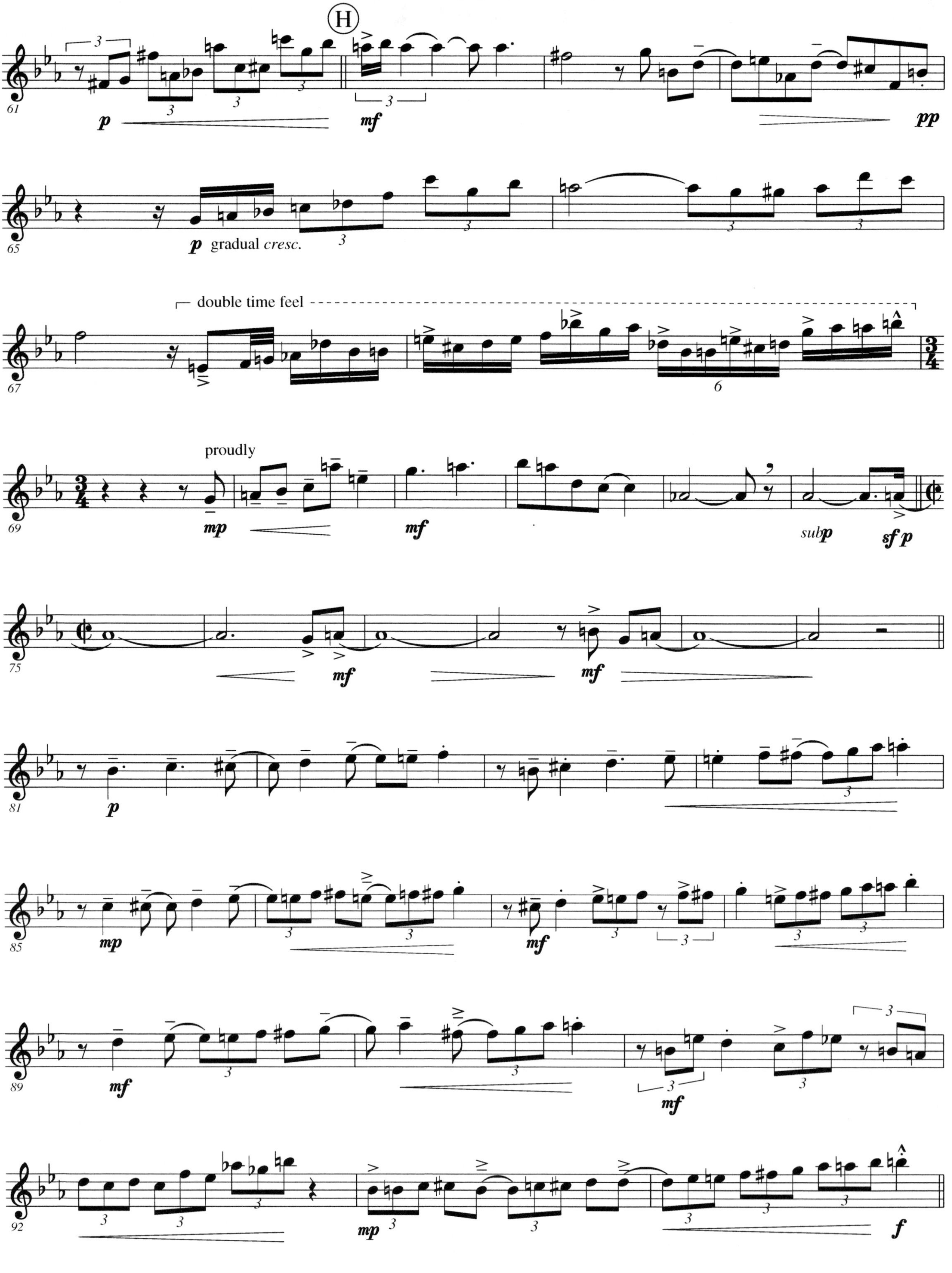

H
double time feel
proudly
gradual cresc.

TENOR SAX 1 page 3 - Thaddeus
vamp until cue
on cue
mf
tr
tr
tr
3
3

Thaddeus

TENOR SAX 2

JERRY DODGION

TENOR SAX 2 page 3 - Thaddeus
vamp until cue
on cue
tr
mf
tr
tr
3

Thaddeus

BARITONE SAX

JERRY DODGION

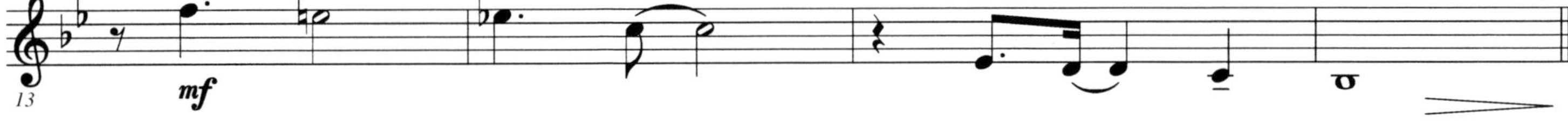

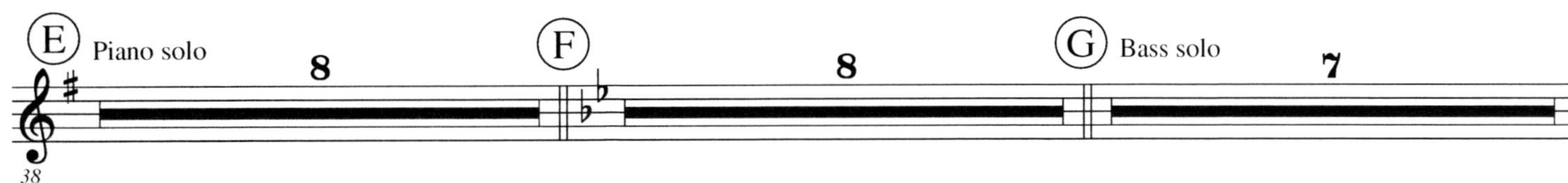

engraved by Osho Endo

H
p
mf
pp
p gradual cresc.
double time feel
6
3/4
proudly
3/4
mp
5
mf
(b)
sub. p
sfp
C
mf
mf
p
mp
3
3
mf
3
3
mf
3
3
mf
3
3
3
3
3
3
3
f
mp

vamp until cue
on cue
tr
mf
tr
tr
tr
3
3
2

Gmaj7 Gbmaj7 Fmaj7 Emaj7 Ebmaj7 A7#5(b9)
Fmaj7/G Emaj7/F#
Ebmaj7/F F7(b9) Ebmaj7 Dm7 Cm7 Bbmaj7 A7
F
Dm7b5 Dbmaj7 Db7#5 (b9) C7#5(b9) Bm7b5 Bbmaj7 Abmaj7 Dbmaj7 C7#5(b9)
Fm9/Bb Em9/A Ebm9/Ab Ab7(b9) Gbmaj7 Fm7 Ebm7 Db
Bass solo
G
Bbdim(maj7) Bdim(maj7) Cdim(maj7) C#dim(maj7)
B7 Bb7 A7 Ab7 Gm F#9(13)
play
p 8vb

H
with Bass
double time feel
with saxes
mf
Alto 1 cue
mp
mf
8vb
8vb
gradual cresc.
8vb
Bass cue
8vb

PIANO page 4 - Thaddeus
vamp until cue
on cue (saxes)
(5)
mf
(6)
Bass cue (8vb)
Bass cue (8vb)
Solo
ff
saxes cue
pedal
2
let ring
no cut off
mf

Thaddeus

engraved by Osho Endo

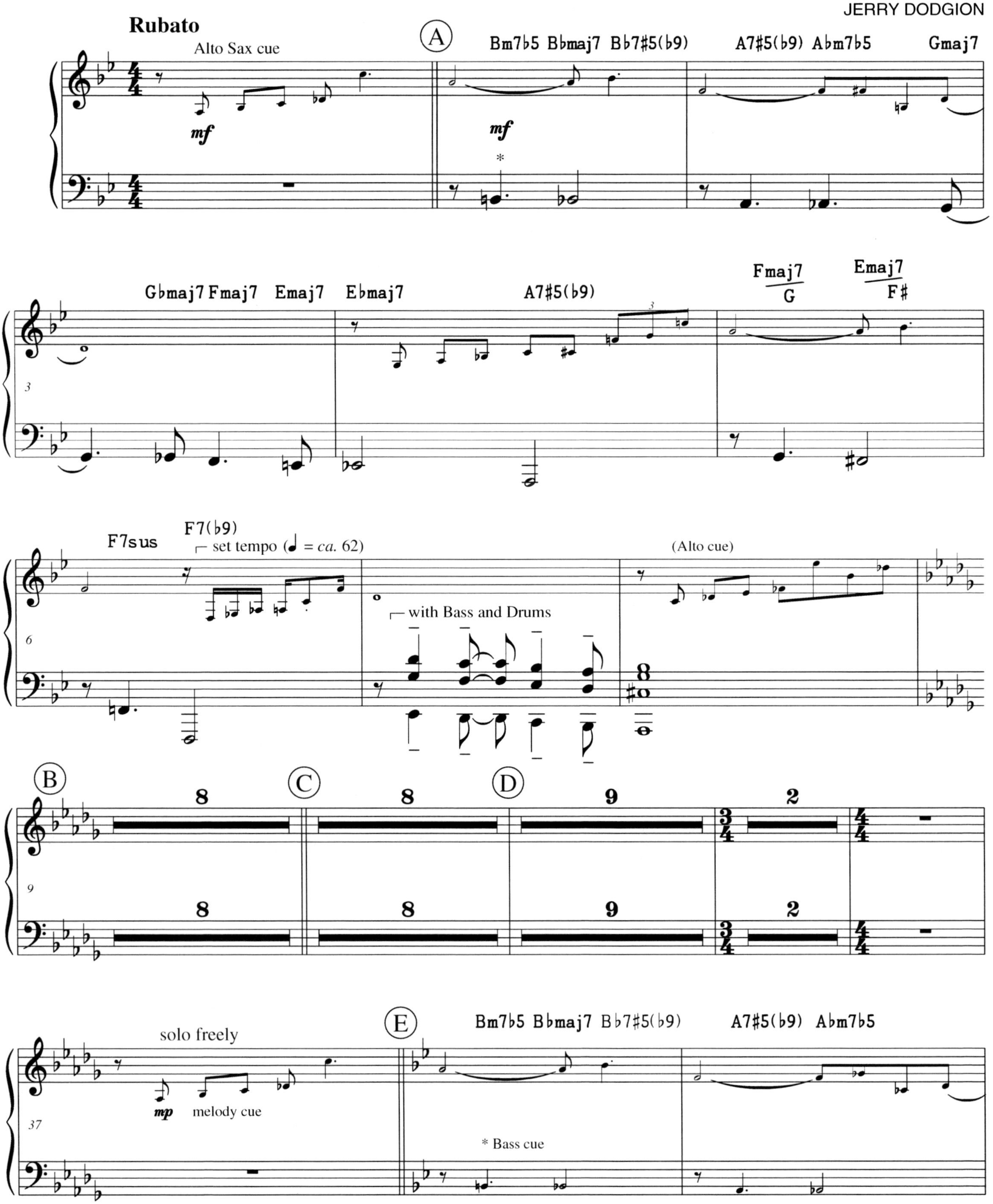

Recorded on THE JOY OF SAX / Jerry Dodgion (Love and Smiles Music LSM 101)
BASS
Thaddeus
set tempo (♩ = ca. 62)
JERRY DODGION 
Rubato
A
5
with Piano and Drums
(Alto 1 cue 8vb)
Alto 1 and Piano
Alto 1 cue
mf
B
3
3
3
(♭)
3
pp
mf
2
C
3
3
3
3
8va
loco
3
3
6
D
3
6
pp
with saxes
3
3
3
3
double time feel
2
3/4
4/4
mp
pp
sfz
Piano solo
E
*
Bm7♭5   B♭maj7   B♭7#5   (♭9)   A7#5(♭9)   A♭m7♭5   Gmaj7   G♭maj7 Fmaj7 Emaj7   E♭maj7   A7#5(♭9)
mf
Fmaj7   Emaj7   E♭maj7   F7(♭9)   E♭maj7 Dm7   Cm7   B♭maj7 A7
 G   F#   F
* suggested rhythmic approach to accompany soloist
Copyright © 1988, 2003 SECOND FLOOR MUSIC
International Copyright Secured   All Rights Reserved   Made in U.S.A.
engraved by Osho Endo

F
Dm7b5 Dbmaj7 Db7#5 (b9)
C7#5(b9) Bm7b5
Bbmaj7
Abmaj7 Dbmaj7 C7#5(b9)
46
Fm9/Bb Em9/A Ebm9/Ab
Ab7(b9)
Gbmaj7 Fm7 Ebm7
Db
solo (melody)
50
G
Bbdim(maj7)
Bdim(maj7)
Cdim(maj7)
C#dim(maj7)
54
B7 Bb7 A7 Ab7
Gm
F#9(13)
Bbm7b5
58
mp
H
62
pp
with saxes
65
mf
double time feel
mf
Alto 1 cue
69
mp
pp
75
mf
mf
81
gradual cresc.
87

vamp until cue
(mf)
on cue (saxes)
(5)
(6)
3
3
saxes cue
with Piano
Piano cue
2
mf
93
97
101
105
109
115
119
123
127
132

Recorded on THE JOY OF SAX / Jerry Dodgion (Love and Smiles Music LSM 101)

Thaddeus

DRUMS
JERRY DODGION

Rubato
A
with Piano and Bass
Alto 1 cue
brushes
Alto 1 and Piano
set tempo (♩ = ca. 62)
mf
(Alto cue)
B
pp
mp
C
D
pp
double time feel
E
Piano solo
*
Piano pick up
p
p
* suggested rhythmic approach to accompany soloist
engraved by Osho Endo

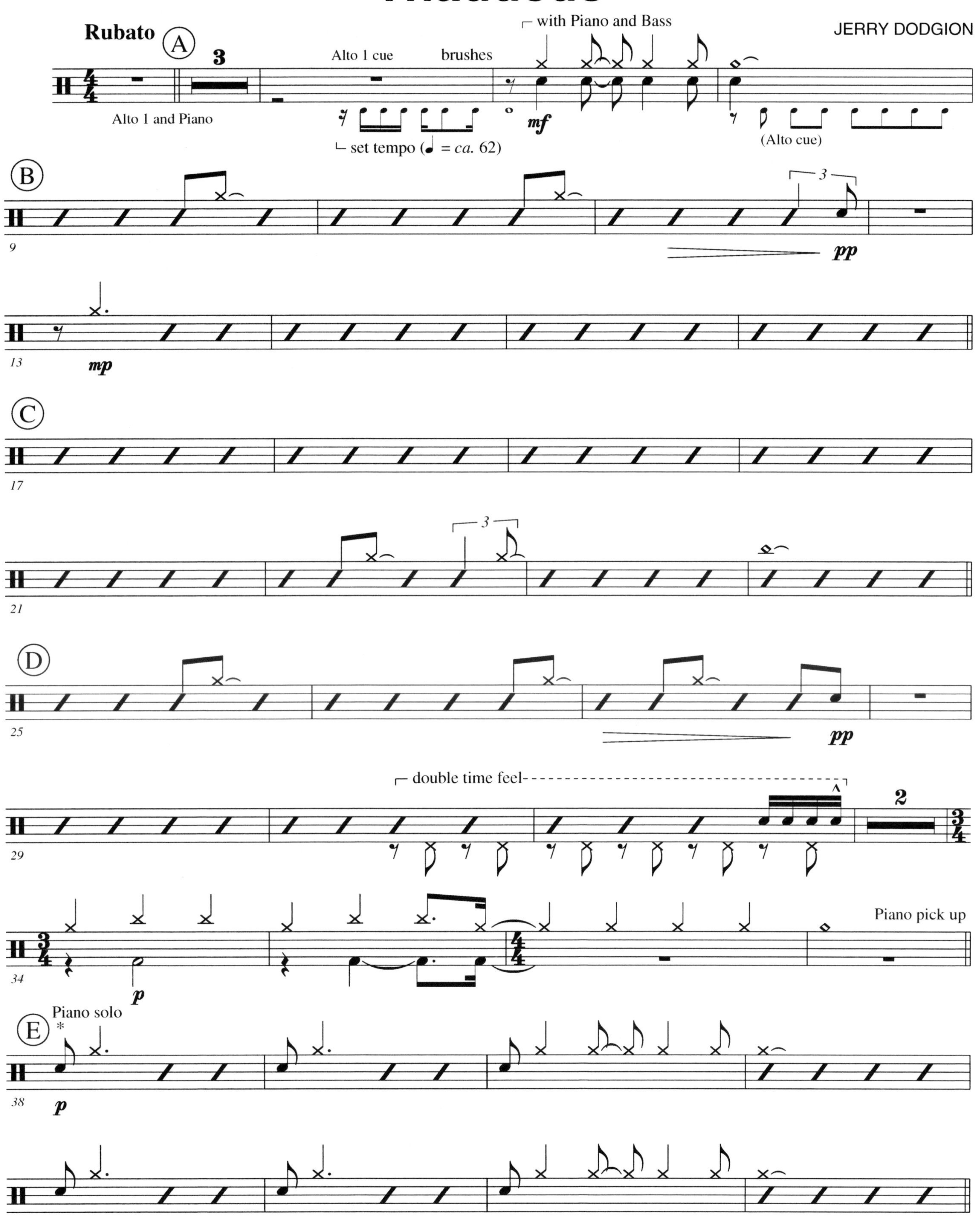

F
46
50
G
Bass solo
54
58
H
62
pp
double time feel
3
4
66
to sticks
3
4
69
Alto 1 cue
p
"time" on hi-hat
75
81
gradual cresc.
85

89
93
mf
vamp until cue
97
on cue (saxes)
(5)
101
3
106
(6)
"time" on hi-hat
109
117
121
"time" continues on hi-hat
125
let ring
no cut off
4
130
Piano cue
Piano and Bass
mf